MANTIS SQUAD
REBORN

MANTIS SQUAD
SQUAD
REBORN

A POETIC NOVEL

by **GORDON BOSTIC**

PR▲MIX
PUBLISHING
THE WRITE CHOICE

Primix Publishing
East Brunswick Office Evolution
1 Tower Center Boulevard, Ste 1510
East Brunswick, NJ 08816
www.primixpublishing.com
Phone: 1-800-538-5788

Published by Primix Publishing: 11/25/2025

ISBN: 979-8-89194-575-3(sc)
ISBN: 979-8-89194-576-0(e)

Library of Congress Control Number: 2025925230

Any people depicted in stock imagery provided by iStock are models, and such images are being used for illustrative purposes only.

Certain stock imagery © iStock.

Because of the dynamic nature of the Internet, any web addresses or links contained in this book may have changed since publication and may no longer be valid. The views expressed in this work are solely those of the author and do not necessarily reflect the views of the publisher, and the publisher hereby disclaims any responsibility for them.

Contents

After Their Ordeal

Once freed from the facility
Their lives they tried reclaim.
Though as result of their training
Nothing had seemed the same.

When to their parents they returned,
Their parents saw the change.
No longer were they teenagers
But more mature and strange.

For gone was the frivolity
That marked the teenage years.
They seemed to be emotionless
Devoid of laughs or tears.

They all had struggled to adjust
Following their ordeal.
Sometimes they tried to tell themselves
That none of it was real.

The sisterhood that they'd once known
They found refused to fade.
As they tried to put behind them
The people Blank had made.

Though they'd chosen separate paths
They all had kept in touch.
The bond they'd built had been maintained
As it had meant so much.

Although a distance was maintained
Where they could not be tracked.
For they feared if they had gathered
They'd surely be attacked.

But they had made one exception
When Kat and Lynn were wed.
For in light of that occasion
They put aside their dread.

Big Brother's Watching

The government had breathed a sigh
When they had disappeared.
For it could not protect itself
From those it engineered.

Although it had been tracking them,
It had not wished them harm.
It wished to know their whereabouts
But not raise an alarm.

They'd proven more than capable
Of exacting a toll.
It had no wish engaging those
That it could not control.

Big Brother had been watching them
As enemies of note.
They'd proven more than dangerous
Though pre-emptive, remote.

It thought it may have need of them
As trainers all were killed.
But prospects of recruiting them
Left it a little chilled.

Damaged Goods

Skye thought that they were damaged goods
As no love had they found.
Only Kat and Lynn seemed happy
But those two had been bound.

Jade had become somewhat reckless
Now Pete was lost to her.
She had not found another man
That her love she'd confer.

The rest had failed relationships
As they could not commit.
They each developed trust issues
Though they, themselves, close-knit.

For they had seen what Jade went through
After Peter had died.
The pain that she experienced
Could not have been denied

The horrors they experienced
Had left them a bit scared.
Where they had shunned relationships
Believing them too hard.

Then objects of a government
That showed them no respect.
Where politicians' promises
Were all they could expect.

Where anger and hostility
Was all they came to prize.
Whose families were torn apart
Under a sleazy guise.

Viewed nothing more than animals
To be brainwashed and trained.
Who had been stripped of dignity
And punished if complained.

The Major and Doctor Cross

While the Major and Doctor Cross
Had not seen eye to eye.
At least Cross was not a sadist
Which Blank could not deny.

While Cross claimed he'd no agenda
In secrets he'd invest.
The Major had not trusted him
Despite what he professed.

For Cross possessed a checkered past
Where boundaries he'd skirt.
His work was all he cared about
Despite whom it may hurt.

It's rumored he's unethical
But nothing had been proved.
So the Major clearly wondered
How Cross had been approved.

The Major a man of honor
Who could not understand
The true purpose of a project
That seemed could not be canned.

Their New Reality

If any knew about their plight
No report ever filed.
It seemed the project was hushed up
And witnesses exiled.

It never made the headline news
As though story was quashed.
It had ignored the evidence
Or evidence was squashed.

Although rumors had run rampant
The government denied
That there'd been some special project
That it had tried to hide.

It was like it never happened
As no one would admit
Who may have been responsible
Or may have known of it.

For they were merely teenagers
With overactive minds.
Who dreamt up a conspiracy
As if they're masterminds.

That was their new reality
They were forced to accept.
For no one believed their story
As secret it was kept.

Issues

Jill acknowledged they had issues
That had not been resolved.
Which through their incarceration
Those issues had evolved.

While Kat and Lynn had seemed happy
As they'd each other found.
The rest of them had shown some signs
Their lives were still fogbound.

Though Jill and Skye were not okay,
The others sparked concern.
They all had seen the change in Chris
That had marked her downturn.

She'd grown sullen and defensive
Which had not been like her.
She, too, had, been acting pensive
Where questions she'd defer.

Brie fed up with all the doting
That to her men had shown.
She rarely had a moment's peace
As she's rarely alone.

She had grown to be standoffish
And often wore disguise.
For she, too, had grown resentful
Of each man's roving eyes.

Jade had grown to be short-tempered
Due to a lack of sleep.
For every time she closed her eyes
In thoughts of Pete would creep.

She never spoke about her loss
Though it had hit her hard.
But it seemed that she'd grown reckless
To safety disregard.

Skye, Jill saw, had grown aggressive
And seemed to have no fear.
She'd become antagonistic
Where threats met with a sneer.

Jill, too, had felt a sense of loss
For what from her they stole.
Her dreams and plans went up in smoke
Which took from her a toll.

She'd not believed the changes good
But with them forced to deal.
It seemed their issues hardened them
To where they could not feel.

Perhaps Blank had more influence
Than they had ever thought.
It seemed that they internalized
The lessons that Blank taught.

Now from their parents all estranged
As they could not reclaim
The pieces of a former life
As they were not the same.

Jill's Mother's Secret

Jill's father caught her by surprise
And fell on bended knee.
He begged her to come home with him
Where she'd be truly free.

He said her mother was not well
Whose final wish had been
To have her daughter close to her
And hug her once again.

Her mother knew of the project
As she had played a part
In development of concept
But not right from the start.

Though she claimed she had no knowledge
That they would come for Jill.
Her mother begged for forgiveness
For part that she'd fulfill.

They had tricked her in believing
It served the common good.
But when the truth had been revealed
Was when she understood

She had abandoned the project
And swore to shut it down.
They ruined her reputation
And made her seem a clown.

When Jill told her she forgave her,
Her mother's eyes had closed.
Jill watched her mother slip away
To in death be composed.

Jill's Lament

When Skye found her, Jill was crying
But Skye had not known why.
When she asked Jill tried to tell her
Though gibberish flew by.

She'd never seen Jill so distraught
Which caused Skye some concern.
Skye moved to try to comfort her
And of her distress learn.

When Jill at last composed herself
To Skye apologized.
She'd not known what came over her
As shame she'd not disguised.

They merely had been teenage girls
When they had first been seized.
Where all that's happened afterwards
Had worsened by degrees.

They'd been victims of circumstance
Beyond theirs to control.
Where they'd claim their mind and bodies
Then rob them of their soul.

For they tried to make them killers
As will they tried to break.
But the lives that they had taken
They had been forced to take.

Not one of them had asked for it
But forced against their will.
A destiny chosen for them
They'd force them to fulfill.

They were meant to be alluring
And then strike like a snake.
Trained to be perfect assassins
Who'd bend, but would not break.

But the training that was hardest
Was learning to seduce.
To some it seemed unnatural,
At least, that's the excuse.

To find her mother part of it
Had truly been a shock.
There's not much more that she could take
As tears she could not block.

Jill called out to the universe
But she got no reply.
It seemed that God abandoned them
While left to wonder why.

Brie's Dilemma

When Lynn had stumbled onto Brie,
She thought Brie looked depressed.
But when Lynn tried to question her
There's nothing Brie confessed.

Then, suddenly, Brie opened up
As tears began to flow.
If a man should come to love her,
How would she ever know?

For men were putty in her hands
Who would grovel and fawn.
Her curse she could not understand,
Why to her men were drawn?

So, if someone should catch her eye
How would she really know
If true love she had discovered
Or her gift brought him low?

Lynn tried her best to sympathize
But really had no clue.
For Kat was who had claimed her heart
And she was faithful to.

Where Errors were Ignored

The facts that Cross had not been told
Had led Cross to believe
This was an opportunity
For greatness to achieve.

The project Cross was to revive,
They said at first had failed.
The leadership not strong enough
As all the subjects bailed.

He was not told of the revolt
Nor trainers had been killed.
The knowledge they thought of no use
As goals went unfulfilled.

Though Mantis Squad was the result
No threat had they become.
Instead, they had gone underground
As they'd not been heard from.

They wished he'd start with a clean slate
Where errors were ignored.
What was the chance that history
Would truly be encored?

So, Cross was left to his designs
To see the project through.
While knowing he's the only one
To whom they could turn to.

Jade and Chris

While Chris and Jade were never close,
They still thought they were friends.
Though secrets shared a rarity
Their trust had known no ends.

A bond born in captivity
Was what the two had earned.
When times grew truly difficult
Jade to whom Chris had turned.

Demands that had been placed on them
Were unjust and unfair.
But they supported each other
Throughout the whole affair.

When Jade lost Pete, Chris had been there
To offer Jade support.
And it was Chris who shared Jade's grief
But tears did not report.

The trust they shared had been intense
And was unshakeable.
Two friends who had stood side by side
And proved unbreakable.

The One Who Hed Been Blessed

It seemed Skye was the only one
Who thought that she'd been blessed.
She treasured her ability
Where can't be second guessed.

She had always been perceptive
In things she'd come to know.
She rarely needed evidence
To know that things were so.

To find someone could lie to her
Had been a rarity.
As people were an open book
She read with clarity.

She truly thought she had been blessed
With gift that she received.
For in depth of her perception
She was hard to deceive.

Jill's Visitor

His name was Major Burberry
That showed up at Jill's door.
Who said he'd a proposition
He wanted to explore.

The Mantis Project to begin
Where trainers were a need.
He'd heard rumors of their exploits
And wished to test their greed.

He told her they could name their price
And conditions could state.
Their expertise what was desired
To warriors create.

The man clearly had been clueless
To what they had been through.
He'd dared to come into her house
As though payback was due.

Jill had stared in stunned amazement
The man had been so bold.
She could kill him in an instant
If she'd been truly cold.

Jill told the man to go away
For he possessed no clue

Of things that had been done to them
Nor what they had been through.

There was no amount of money
That could buy their return.
The fact the project was revived
Was their only concern.

As soon as he had left her house
Jill next had texted Skye.
She could not believe the nonsense
And umbrage of the guy.

Questions Without Answers

Why the questions had no answers
It had not ascertained.
Who was the one responsible
That project entertained?

For the fallout a disaster
It had worked hard to crush.
As the project was unsanctioned
And thus, had been hush-hush.

It seemed someone diverted funds
Though no one had known who.
The whole thing had proved a nightmare
That few were privy to.

He'd then tricked the military
To the project defend.
And even fooled superiors
To on it over spend.

He'd secured the facility
And then had hired a staff.
Though he had no authority,
Most probably a gaffe.

The operation was covert,
To say the very least.
For no one, it seemed, had a clue
To nature of the beast.

Unable to find evidence
To who deserved the blame.
It had no choice but cover-up
And thus, avoid the shame.

It thought that it had put in place
Restrictions to prevent
All the shady shenanigans
That none could circumvent.

But it now became apparent
Someone had found a Crack.
With a project instituted
That it could not walk back.

Jill's Mental State

Skye worried that Jill's mental state
Was not what it should be.
It had seemed that she'd lost focus
And, maybe, clarity.

It seemed her mind was miles away
When to her Skye would speak.
As though Skye's words were lost to her
And she'd grown truly meek.

As if she carried the world's weight
And weight had wore her down.
Jill's smile had made her face light up
But now showed only frown.

Though Skye believed that Jill was torn
By matters of the heart.
There were two paths that called to her
And with one she must part.

Pandora's Box

Burberry was an idiot
Who had not understood
Pandora's box had been unleashed
Which for him was not good.

He'd unwittingly informed her
Her greatest fear was true.
The project was to be revived
Which she'd not let them do.

The project reprehensible
In purpose and design.
And those who're at the heart of it
To evil would align.

The ones who'd chosen to hire Cross
Neglected to reveal
They had been down this path before
From which they still would reel.

If what Burberry alluded
Even remotely true.
The others should be notified
And course chose to pursue.

The Threat

The government would not admit
The threat the Squad had posed.
For any mention that it made
The project was exposed.

It had little chance to stop them
If an objective found.
So, even with its surveillance
Its worries would compound.

It had feared that they were monsters
That Blank dared to create.
Who'd found killing a compulsion
That they could never sate.

The government would have no qualms
In taking each one out
But it had feared what was required
And cost of the payout.

It also feared attacking one
Would just rally the rest.
Who'd proved to be unstoppable
Against its very best.

The only choice it seemed it had
Was not to get them riled.
The prospect of confrontation
Had left it quite beguiled.

The Reception

The reception had proved ideal
For them to meet and talk.
With less chance to be overheard
And people would not gawk.

Skye then told them she'd discovered
The project was restored.
Somehow new funding was acquired
Which left the others floored.

She'd not known if they're targeted
Or they'd build a new team.
Whomever was responsible
Their soul they'd not redeem.

Jade said she thought they'd wrecked the place
Beyond human repair.
Skye said with funds available
They really did not care.

They had thought they'd been forgotten
But that was not the case.
The government kept tabs on them
As movements it would trace.

Till she had more information,
Skye warned them to lay low.
She had no wish to worry them
But thought they ought to know.

The Secret

Skye then looked at all their faces
When she began to laugh.
They all were foolish to believe
Their secret not a gaffe.

She had known they still were training
Though each one on their own.
And all of them had been remiss
To think Skye had not known.

Perhaps they'd been apart too long
Where they'd too soon forgot
Each had unique abilities
Though Skye's was hard to spot.

They all then shared that knowing grin
That secrets were a waste.
For Skye had known each one of theirs
The moment each was faced.

Chris's Anxiety

Chris would not go through it again
And told the others so.
She still had nightmares of the place
That she could not let go.

Kat looked at Chris, then took her hand
And told her they all knew.
They shared in her experience
And had been damaged, too.

But they survived it as a team,
As team they had become.
The fear of that experience
They had to overcome.

They could not let some other girls
Go through what they went through.
This insanity had to end
As only they could do.

Chris looked around her sisterhood
And knew that it was true.
When Jill would say the time was right
She'd do what she must do.

The seven of them then group hugged
To sisterhood affirm.
Whatever was their destiny
It likely was short-term.

All Eyes Turned to Jill

The question now was what to do
With Intel that they had.
Although there's little they had known
What was known had been bad.

They had to know with certainty
How far ahead they'd planned.
And who they may have targeted
That they'd wished to command.

It seemed that Jill was still the one
To whom all eyes would turn
Whenever there was any doubt
Or some major concern.

For most her life it'd been that way
Though she had not known why.
Where even as a little girl
On her, friends would rely.

Perhaps it was her high IQ
That allowed her to see
The solution to a puzzle
With such crisp clarity.

Where in every situation
In which she was involved
All other eyes had turned to her
For it to be resolved.

Information Gathering

The plan that Jill laid out for them
Was clever and direct.
And something that the government
Would not come to expect.

Their first incursion must be quick
And could not leave a trace.
Their mission was to find the files
And then exit the place.

They needed to find what they planned
And had far they had come.
Then, too, they must identify
The list they would choose from.

If it would not come after them
Then others in harm's way.
They'd need its list of candidates
If they're to save the day.

But to find that information
They would have to invade
The depths of the facility
Where Mantis Squad was made.

They knew it could be dangerous
But options had been few.
The project, they thought, must be stopped
And it was overdue.

They chose to keep Chris out of it
Due to her fragile state.
She'd be a danger to them all
If she should hesitate.

The Break-in

Their entry was undetected.
They knew the place by heart.
From every secret passageway
To where patrols would start.

Brie created a diversion
That lured the guards away.
After which Jade breached the steel door
That led to the hallway.

Lynn created an illusion
The door had still been closed.
Where the truth of their intrusion
Not readily exposed.

Then the others in their party
Had headed for the stairs
Which led to the command center,
The home of their affairs.

They searched through filing cabinets
Recording with their phones
Every piece of evidence
As though creating clones.

Meanwhile Jill accessed computers
To find files to offload
Of everything that's relevant
Which she'd simply download.

When they were done, their steps retraced
Then exited the place.
Their operation went as planned
With nothing left to trace.

Though Brie had found it difficult
To take leave from the guards.
Till she, finally, relented
And accepted their cards.

Tracked

The government kept track of them
Which none of them had known.
Because it had created them,
The problem was its' own.

They'd proven more than capable
In acts of sabotage.
And never appeared hesitant
To plague its entourage.

Though they'd been dormant for a while
It would not take the chance
There'd be something to alert them
To wake them from their trance.

They'd proven they were dangerous
To where they were a blight.
But they, too, were superior
If drawn into a fight.

The Mantis Squad was a mistake
It had meant to correct.
But its options were limited
With what it may effect.

It had no wish to provoke them
Nor bring their plans to light.
For it feared the consequences
If they, it should incite.

Because it had created them
It knew what they could do.
The Mantis Squad was a mistake
That it could not undo.

The Home Invasion

The knock had startled Lynn and Kat
As it was very late.
Kat told Lynn to just ignore it
Believing they'd not wait.

Then men in black crashed through the door
Who were clear in intent.
Their mission clearly their demise
Which had been evident.

The government thought them elite
But too soon had forgot
The Mantis Squad a step beyond
In how skilled they had fought.

The men in black caught by surprise
With how quick Kat had struck.
She'd swiftly subdued two of them
Who'd not had time to duck.

Another fired a shot at Lynn
Whom he had somehow missed.
The bullet, though, shattered a vase
Which, truly, left Lynn pissed.

Lynn grabbed the bottom of the vase
And hurled it 'cross the room.
The shard had hit him in the throat
To instantly spell doom.

Another bullet whizzed by Kat
As she had grabbed his gun.
Then smashed him with the butt of it
Before he'd chance to run.

The men in black made their retreat
As quickly as they'd come.
They found that they had been outmatched
And swiftly overcome.

While they surveyed all the damage,
Kat said it could be worse.
As Kat lifted from the rubble
What was her brand-new purse.

9-1-1

A neighbor had called 9-1-1
When a disturbance heard.
Ms. Martin had not known them well
But noises were absurd.

Though Jill and Skye first to arrive
When they received the news.
And thankful that they were okay
Though Kat a minor bruise.

Next the responding officer
Had arrived on the scene.
Where he'd seen there'd been a struggle
But not what it may mean.

The officer announced he's Rick
And asked it they're okay.
Then he asked them what had happened
As damage he'd survey.

Kat said the men had all worn masks
To hide identities.
They'd simply stormed into their house
Shouting unpleasantries.

But for each question he had asked
They had tried to deflect.
As if the ones responsible
They had wished to protect.

While their friends were less than helpful
In claiming they'd no clue.
It had seemed a home invasion
Which bad people will do.

Rick thought their answers made no sense
But had no wish to grill.
The only thing that caught his eye
The couple's friend named Jill.

Before he left, he asked of Jill
If number she'd provide.
In case he'd need to follow-up
Or suspects had been spied.

Jill's Discoveries

The information went with Jill
So, it she could review.
She prayed they'd collected something
That would provide a clue.

Jill had found the files encrypted
But with Skye's help revealed
All the secrets of the project
The government concealed.

She found the Major still in charge
Of its security.
While there'd been a new Director
Of the facility.

The new Director's name was Cross
Who had a shady past.
With research that's unauthorized
Prior jobs did not last.

Repairs to the facility
Had come at some great cost.
The fact funds were available
Had not on her been lost.

Jill found a lot of useful things
Though some, too, brought concern.
The project they'd revitalize
Would take a stricter turn.

Jill saw eight girls were targeted
Which they'd seek to prevent.
So horrors they experienced
These girls could circumvent.

From the Intel that they'd gathered
Jill hoped she could discern
The date and time of the assaults
That they could overturn.

Though the last thing Jill had noticed
New detectors installed.
That knowledge truly was a shock
And had left her appalled.

Skye told Jill she'd confirmation
The government had known
They'd been in the facility
And had not gone alone.

The Phone Call

The phone at first had startled her
When it began to ring.
For it had caught her by surprise
As call not expecting.

Jill answered to find it was Rick
Who wished to ask her out.
He told her that she intrigued him
Though Jill was racked with doubt.

Jill was unsure how to respond
As she'd been caught off guard.
She'd not realized he'd noticed her
Nor had gained his regard.

Jill looked to Skye for her advice
Who told her she should go.
It was a chance to have some fun
Like she'd known years ago.

The Choice

Their meeting had been clandestine
As Skye had said it should.
She'd gained access to some Intel
She said had not been good.

Jill found that there had been a list
Of those it meant to claim.
A younger group of those like them
The project chose to name.

The horrors they'd experienced
Would all be faced anew.
Where another group subjected
To what they had been through.

Where both Jill and Skye united
In sharing the belief
They could not let it reoccur
But offer them relief.

It's sometimes said that history
Will of itself repeat.
Where lessons that should have been learned
Though people tend to cheat.

There was a choice that must be made
Though options had seemed grim.
For interference dangerous
If they'd try rescue them.

The List

The list of girls Jill uncovered
Had proven quite a find.
They each, too, had abilities
That clearly were defined.

Debbie Lynn they thought clairvoyant
With what she could perceive.
For the things that she detected
Few others could conceive.

Beth was like a human spider
Who could climb anything.
Where any crevice she could use
As up a wall she'd spring.

In Page they had discovered
That she could see at night
Even in the dimmest setting
Or in absence of light.

Kimberly had been much like Skye
Possessing ESP.
She'd been extremely perceptive,
Persuasive if need be.

Dawn had that special quality
As same that Brie possessed.
Men found her irresistible
With affections professed.

Kate's skills were more unusual
Involving taste and smell.
Where both senses had been acute
And proved to serve her wel.

Jasmine was a freak of nature
With reflexes possessed.
She was blessed with cat-like quickness
Beyond what they could test.

Kay was more than an acrobat
In things that she could do.
She, too, was a contortionist
Where pipes she could pass through.

Like them, were inexperienced
With their abilities.
Thus, helpless to defend themselves
Becoming abductees.

Their Cross to Bear

The information Jill had shared
Had come as no surprise.
For they'd been through it all before
And to it had been wise.

Eight girls, Jill said, had been at risk
That they were primed to save
From the things they'd experienced
Which had been more than grave.

Though eight girls had been targeted
There're seven homes to guard.
Two of the girls a set of twins
With separation hard.

With each assigned a family
They were charged to protect.
They'd stop the project at the start
Before it had effect.

They feared they could not save them all
But they'd commit to try.
They each had pledged to save the girls
Even if they must die.

The horrors they experienced
They'd not let reoccur.
Whatever it was they must do
Abductions they'd deter.

If there's anyone to stop them
It was their cross to bear.
For it seemed there were few others
That of it were aware.

The Failed Abduction

It had been in the dead of night
When the raids had been staged.
And all were simultaneous
So, none would be upstaged.

The girl's name had been Debbie Lynn
To whom Skye was assigned.
Jill said that she'd been targeted
But to fate not resigned.

Her parents had been pushed aside
As Debbie they secured.
While their questions went unanswered
As though they'd been censured.

At the moment of their exit
Skye swept into the room.
Demanding they release the girl
Or they'd face certain doom.

Their bodies flew around the room
As if they'd been Mache.
While Skye had seemed to be unscathed
Which the men could not say.

It seemed she knew their every move
Before it had been made.
She'd fought as though a warrior
Who had applied her trade.

They, suddenly, made their retreat
When saw there was no use.
It was a fight they could not win
And tired of the abuse.

Debbie then thanked Skye profusely.
Her parents had as well.
Skye said that she was glad to help
In saving them from hell.

Jade and Kimberly

The men who stormed into their home
Had come for Kimberly.
She had tried to warn her parents
But they ignored her plea.

They had first restrained her parents
So, they'd not interfere.
Though she had tried to ward them off
She's seen she'd spawned no fear.

Then, suddenly, the men had froze
As Jade stood in the door.
It seemed that she had just appeared
And could not be ignored.

The men in black had clearly flinched
The moment they saw Jade.
They knew of what she's capable
And clearly were afraid.

Jade told them she felt generous
And offered chance to leave.
Though should they ignore her offer,
She guaranteed they'd greave.

They paused as though considering
The offer that was made.
Then one of them had broken ranks
As he had charged at Jade.

Jade dropped him like a ton of bricks
Then stomped and broke his arm.
The others seemed more hesitant
In racing into harm.

Jade told Kimberly to join her
Which Kim had raced to do.
If the men wanted Kimberly
It's Jade they must go through.

Jade told the men that they should leave
While they still had the chance.
The men looked to one another
And then at Jade would glance.

Next, they helped their fallen comrade
In regaining his feet.
And while the men had stared at Jade,
They made a quick retreat.

As they left, Kimberly hugged her
And thanked her for her aid.
Then when her parents had been freed,
A fuss they also made.

The Encounter with Jasmine

When front and back doors had been breached
Jasmine had tried to run.
Her parents had been out that night
So, protection she'd none.

The men armed with tranquilizers
But could not draw a bead.
It seemed Jasmine was everywhere
While threats she would not heed.

She heard the gun as it was fired
Then dart flew by her head.
Next one of them the dart had struck
Who crumpled as if dead.

When Jill arrived upon the scene
She, at first, was amused.
For Jasmine had bewildered them
Where tormentors confused.

Jill could see the men's frustration
Jasmine's not yet detained.
Every time they'd thought her cornered
She'd proven uncontained.

They'd grown so tired of chasing her
They had no will to fight.
When Jill had ordered them to leave
They quickly took to flight.

Then with Jasmine Jill had waited
Till parents had returned.
While Jasmine revealed what happened
Her parents were concerned.

Jill had told them that she doubted
Those men would dare come back.
But she also had assured them
Their travels she would track.

In the meantime, Jill advised them
To keep a watchful eye.
As their daughter was the target
For which they'd chanced to die.

Then she gave them her phone number
And told them they should call
If they saw something suspicious
Or any need at all.

Assessment

The other stories similar
For those who had arrived.
As some of them had been detained
With chance to save deprived.

They could not get to all of them
Despite how hard they tried.
It seemed that fate had intervened
Where efforts were denied.

Though Jill and Jade had found success
The other four had failed.
But not due to lack of effort
Nor because they had bailed.

For Kat and Lynn arrived too late
It had not been their fault.
The Parkway was a parking lot
With progress move and halt.

While Chris and Brie's flights were delayed
They'd not arrived in time
To have staged an intervention
That would have stopped the crime.

They'd prevented three abductions
Though five others were lost.
Which had meant they'd need to find them
Whatever was the cost.

They'd not allow them duplicate
The horrors they had known.
Where, instead, they'd show compassion
Unlike what they were shown.

The Prisoner

One of the men felled by a dart
They'd deftly left behind.
So, when the man had been revived
Skye tried to pick his mind.

For when the men in black had left
Jill quickly had called Skye.
For Jill had gained a prisoner
From whom answers they'd pry.

The one thing Skye had hated most
Were those who'd try to lie.
Who foolish thought she could be tricked
Or truth they could deny.

When Jill pulled Skye off to the side
To ask what Skye had bought.
Skye said she's not a telepath
Who'd every thought had caught.

For she'd found him so corrupted
That every truth he knew
Had been more like a fantasy
From training he'd been through.

Most people were an open book
But he'd been hard to read.
As though the truth was a concept
For which he had no need.

First Date

Jill met Rick at a coffee shop
Where table Rick reserved.
While Skye encouraged her to go
As something she deserved.

She'd forgotten what it felt like
To have again a life.
For in the world she'd come to know
There only had been strife.

As they both engaged in small talk
Rick felt Jill holding back.
For there're questions she deflected
Or answers seemed to lack.

Though clearly not unattractive,
There had been something more
That simply had called out to him
Which he could not ignore.

Rick saw her as a mystery
That he may never solve.
But he would not give up on her
Was something he'd resolve.

When she thanked him for the coffee
As she arose to leave.
Rick asked if they could meet again
A smile he would receive.

Remembrance

The fact the girls had been taken
Had forced Chris to recall
The details of imprisonment
That still made her skin crawl.

She remembered what it felt like
When they had taken her.
With that feeling of hopelessness
That she could not deter.

Where she prayed one day she'd be free
To leave it all behind.
Though worried in the aftermath
How damaged was her mind.

The things that they had planned for her
Required a strength of will.
But in her heart, she had not thought
That she could ever kill.

She even tried delude herself
That none of it was real.
Where she was trapped in a nightmare
That had no great appeal.

While the doubts that seemed to plague her
Could've led to her downfall.
She'd drawn strength from the others
Who had stood proud and tall.

She looked to Jill, and then to Skye
To what she was to do.
For she trusted in their guidance
To help her to pull through.

And they proved true to her belief
Where, now, she had been free.
A debt that she still owed to them,
Though they would disagree.

Cross' Staff and Superior

The Major once tried intercede
Upon the girls' behalf.
Cross warned him to stay out of it
Then pointed to his staff.

His aides were nothing more than thugs
That to Cross were assigned.
Though the Major had no knowledge
To whom Cross was aligned.

The Major disapproved of them
But not his to command.
So, he could only stand and watch
What proved a lawless band.

But he had a superior
Who, clearly, pulled the strings.
For Cross had not been bold enough
To do such evil things.

Cross must have thought he's protected
From any choice he made.
For he had not seemed to worry
Nor showed signs he's afraid.

Someone to Cross superior
Who had the plan approved.
Someone to whom he answered to
The Major wished removed.

The Pain

When Rick unable to reach Jill,
His next call was to Skye.
As though she was Jill's guardian
Though Skye had not known why.

But she found it was annoying
He tried to pull her in.
As if she was a go-between
So, Jill's heart he could win.

Skye thought that Rick was immature
The way he hounded Jill.
For his phone calls were incessant
As her time tried to fill.

Skye had no wish to be involved
But seemed to have no choice.
When Rick came up as the ID.
She wished she had no voice.

She'd not known what Jill saw in him.
To Skye he was a pain.
Although when Skye had dared inquire
Jill found hard to explain.

A Return to Normalcy

Like a return to normalcy
Had been her date with Rick.
Although afraid to get too close
He had been a great pick.

When Skye had asked her how it went
Jill's face had simply beamed.
She said the night was magical
And better than she dreamed.

Jill said that he was nice enough
But she had been afraid.
She could not open up to him
As past upon her weighed.

She worried what he'd think of her
If her past he had known.
Though crimes that she was guilty of
Not exactly her own.

Besides it would be dangerous
To have him close at hand.
For that may place his life at risk.
Which he'd not understand.

So, she vowed to keep her distance
Though her heart disagreed.
Skye thought that he was good for her
But Jill had not agreed.

All to no Avail

It'd not been Rick who tried to call
But rather Kimberly.
There was a van outside her house
Where threat it seemed to be.

They made the trip in record time
As Jill and Skye took turns.
They only stopped to exchange seats
So great were their concerns.

Her parents said some men in black
Had taken Kim away.
The reasons they had come for her
They had refused to say.

While overcome with their concern,
Skye's heart went out to them.
But had not said what she had feared
Believing it too grim.

Skye checked the other families
To find their daughters, too,
Were taken by men dressed in black
Where no answers were due.

Thus, it seemed that prior efforts
Had been to no avail.
The men in black bided their time
Until they could prevail.

The project, now, had all the girls
For whom it showed desire.
Skye and Jill looked to each other
Exchanging scowls of ire.

The Task

The eight girls who had been captured
Doctor Cross had assessed
To depth of their abilities
That each of them possessed.

The girls had huddled together
So great had been their fear.
But Doctor Cross showed no concern
As at them he would sneer.

To him they're nothing more than rats
To be tested and trained.
Their feelings of no consequence
For what he entertained.

It's an army of assassins
That he'd been tasked to build.
Where these girls were the prototypes
Of what he'd come to field.

He'd strip them of identity
And then destroy each soul.
Next each of them would be reborn
To be his to control.

The State of Their Existence

Each day was marked by greater fear
Where if a task they'd fail
The punishment that they'd receive
Would leave them weak and frail.

Each felt that they were soon to break
Or buckle to the strain.
For Cross demanded perfection
Which had become a drain.

The penalties imposed on them
Were truly undeserved.
But they seemed to empower Cross
Although no purpose served.

Each day had proven to be worse
Than was the day before.
As they were given no respite
From their lessons in war.

The limits to which they were pushed
Had truly been unfair.
But Cross claimed he had a schedule
And only halfway there.

True Happiness

Rick had taken Jill to dinner
To mark their second date.
Which proved to be an interlude
That both had thought was great.

She'd never known such joy before
But feared it was a dream.
The fact that Rick had noticed her
Seemed luck to the extreme.

Rick seemed to be an honest man
Who said what he believed.
His thoughts he'd spoken openly
And trust he had achieved.

She thought he was a shining light
Who's too good to be true.
She found her heart would start to race
When he came into view.

The qualities that called to her
Were decency and charm.
His humor was self-defacing
And was hard to alarm.

Jill never had been kissed before
Though found it was a thrill.
While it had come as a surprise
Resistance had been nil.

She'd never known true happiness
As that which she had found.
Which she thought she'd feel forever
As long as Rick's around.

Jill knew that Rick had cared for her
When Brie entered the room.
His attention never wavered
Nor presence he'd consume.

The Team Complete

The new girls thrown in with the rest
To find their team complete.
Though there'd be catching up to do,
No training they'd repeat.

The new girls had been shocked to find
What expectations loomed.
For there was no quarter given
Where all had felt they're doomed.

It seemed that they'd been marked for death
Despite which way it fell.
While meantime in the interim
Their lives a living hell.

They had grown tired of the torment
That each day they had faced.
Whatever good had lived in them
Cross meant to have replaced.

Nothing He could Do

Their training Cross intensified
Perturbed with progress made.
They were not working hard enough
Where schedule was delayed.

Cross told them he'd not tolerate
Their efforts to disguise
Their reluctance to their training
So, shot Page tween the eyes.

The four, remaining, terrified
Of what Cross next may do.
Their sobs were uncontrollable
In fear their deaths were due.

The Major was beside himself
But found his hands were tied.
Cross had clearly been a monster
Which someone wished to hide.

The project clearly out of hand
But nothing could he do.
They'd given Cross complete control
To see the project through.

He saw the tears were genuine
But nothing could he do.
While Cross had seemed oblivious
To what he'd put them through.

The cruelty that Cross had displayed
Had been beyond belief.
But there was nothing he could do
To offer them relief.

Jill's Concerns

She knew that Rick had cared for her,
Perhaps, more than he should.
For he'd known little of her past
And rest prayed never would.

But Jill had quickly grown concerned
What his intentions were.
For as the evening had progressed
His focus was on her.

Jill had felt things were progressing
At much too quick a pace.
While it's true she may be smitten
This not the time nor place.

There was too much Rick had not known
And she had feared to tell.
He was making some assumptions
That may not serve him well.

Jill would admit she'd grown afraid
Of what this may become.
Rick had no clue to who she was
Nor what she had come from.

The Major's Quandary

Although the Major filed complaints
About treatment received.
The Major had grown furious
The girls had been aggrieved.

Cross treated them like animals
Or, maybe, even worse.
For the girls had been degraded
Where the effects adverse.

The Major saw no need for it
And thought that Cross was wrong.
But his objections were ignored
As Cross had been headstrong.

The Major thought mistake was made
When Cross they chose to hire.
Cross teetered on insanity
Whose methods had proved dire.

A dark part of the government
Had been behind it all.
But he'd not the authority
To make a judgment call.

The fact that Cross he had misjudged
Weighed heavy on his mind.
For the bastard was a sadist
Which he was slow to find.

These girls had not deserved this fate
But nothing could he do.
His orders had been very clear
Which he must adhere to.

Second Thoughts

Their rendezvouses grew more frequent
As the days had slipped by.
For Jill enjoyed Rick's company
Though she was unsure why.

While hesitant to be involved
She could not help herself.
For Rick was a terrific guy
Who rarely thought of self.

Jill looked into Rick's eyes and thought
That she could not admit
With depth of feeling held for him
She still could not commit.

Though she thought he was delightful
And a really great guy,
It truly was unfair to him
To know that she may die.

She feared Rick getting serious
Which she could not allow.
So, Jill was having second thoughts
Which caused her furrowed brow.

The Recall

The Major had been notified
That he had been recalled.
He found that Cross lodged a complaint
For which he'd been appalled.

Cross charged the Major interfered
With methods he employed.
Which hampered the development
Of those he had employed.

The Major claimed that Cross had lied.
The girls had been detained.
They had been kidnapped from their homes
While parents were restrained.

The evidence presented them
The hierarchy ignored.
The project had been paramount
With nothing else explored.

The project was assigned to Cross
From which he should stay clear.
For if it should be jeopardized
He'd forfeit his career.

The smirk that Cross had given him
When the Major returned
Had rubbed the Major the wrong way
Where only anger burned.

Jill's Decision

Her decision was a hard one
With which she'd have to live.
At least she knew Rick would be safe
Though he may not forgive.

There was a chance she'd not return
And with that was okay.
For if the project was shutdown
She'd sacrifice all day.

Jill had tried to put behind her
The horrors of her past.
For Rick offered her a future
Her present would contrast.

The decision was difficult
But one she had to make.
Where she felt further involvement
Would be a huge mistake.

The heart may want what it may want
Which sometimes cannot be.
Though prisoner to her desires
She's ruled by destiny.

So, his phone calls she had ignored
And texts she'd not return.
Her choice had nearly broke her heart
With nowhere else to turn.

Until the project was shutdown
Her life was not her own.
There was a mission to fulfill
And light that must be shone.

The project reprehensible
In purpose and design.
They swore to put an end to it
Though plan to yet outline.

What Page had Said

Each night they cried themselves to sleep
So desperate their plight.
There was no chance of an escape
As tunnel held no light.

There would be none to rescue them,
Cross told them every day,
They might as well resign themselves
That they were here to stay.

Page told them that the day would come
When from Cross they'd be free.
It's then they'd have their reckoning
Where victim would be he.

Although the girls were unaware
Their quarters had been bugged.
Where Cross had heard her every word
As she had been unplugged.

So, everything that Page declared
Went straight to Cross's ear.
Where Cross believed Page was a threat
That he may come to fear.

The Confrontation

Rick wondered what it was he'd done
That his calls she ignored.
He'd seen the way she'd looked at him
And her smile he adored.

So, he'd been stunned Jill shut him down
And gave no reason why.
He thought that he was good for her
A fact she can't deny.

Jill had feared the confrontation
She knew was sure to come.
She knew Rick deserved some answers
As to what she'd become.

Jill tried to face the doubts she felt
But they had been too great.
She had not been prepared for this
But this had seemed her fate.

It seemed, sometimes, to prove your love
You have to set it free.
With what she was to undertake
Perhaps it's meant to be.

Jill wished to save him from himself
For she was damage goods.
She thought Rick had deserved better
Than deal with her falsehoods.

Rick said he'd not give up on her
As his heart had been hers.
But tired of all the secrecy
And questions she defers.

The Heart May Want

The heart may want what it may want
An old proverb may say.
But romance was not meant for Jill,
Thus, must be pushed away.

Although her thoughts would turn to him
When she would least expect.
Rick tried to call her all the time
But calls she would reject.

She wished that it was different
Yet, her reality
Was one destined for loneliness
From which she'd not be free.

Jill wished that Rick would take the hint
And just leave her alone.
But persistent Rick had proven
So, she turned off her phone.

The Shock of Page's Death

They all were shocked by Page's death
As none had seen the need.
She worked as hard as anyone
Yet, life she did concede.

It seemed that Cross had breached a line
He never should have crossed.
He saw the way they looked at him
Where fear, it seemed, they'd lost.

Their eyes revealed the hate they'd felt
And could no longer hide.
Where all they had looked forward to
Was hearing Cross had died.

The effort that they now put forth
Brought worry to his aides.
No longer frightened little girls
Fearful of his tirades.

They trained with new intensity
As though a purpose gained.
They each had grown belligerent
With hatred unrestrained.

The threat of death enveloped them
To where they'd ceased to care.
As death was something to embrace
For those who weren't aware.

The Universe Cried Out

Skye had awakened with a start
Feeling something was wrong.
As they had planned for their assault,
The planning took too long.

The universe cried out to her
That an injustice done.
She wished she had more clarity
But found there had been none.

Skye felt the anguish they had felt
But had been left to guess
The nature of the incident
That they were to witness.

She could feel their anxiety
And with that feeling knew
One held in the facility
Had found her death come due.

Skye told the others what she felt
Where they had all agreed
The time for planning was long past
With action now their need.

Foreshadowing

They no longer were the victims
But were the hand of God.
For that was what they trained them for
And, thus, the Mantis Squad.

They no longer had been children
Who could be bossed around.
Instead, they had been highly trained
Whose skills had been profound.

The only way evil survives
Is letting it run free.
Where they recognize its presence
But pretend not to see.

Chris said it's time to lock and load
As Judgment Day was here.
The Mantis Squad they'd given birth
This day they'd come to fear.

As each of them had armed themselves
They knew what was at stake.
The hostages that were inside
They each vowed to retake.

This time they'd be expecting them
But payback had come due.
The death of the facility
Was truly overdue.

Where was Their Rescue?

While they prayed that they'd be rescued,
No rescue, yet, had come.
Each day was another nightmare
To which they would succumb.

They were never shown a kindness,
In fact, treatment was cruel.
Whatever goal was set for them
They could not overrule.

Mistakes they would not tolerate
Where punishment came swift.
To be placed in solitary
The girls viewed as a gift.

Debbie Lynn had grown furious
With promise Skye had made.
Who'd said that she'd be there for her
Though rescue seemed waylaid.

They wondered why none came for them,
In this, their time of need.
Had families abandoned them
As to this they agreed?

While prayers seemed to be ignored
To save them from their plight.
Perhaps it simply was a case
Out of mind, out of sight.

An Error to be Rectified

Jill had one thing to accomplish
Before the planned assault.
An error to be rectified
Where she had been at fault.

Sometimes your past, you can't outrun
And so, it was with Jill.
She felt the truth she owed to Rick
Before her goal fulfill.

A little bit of honesty
Was all that Rick required.
And since Jill's future in question
In secrets she was mired.

She told Rick of their cruel ordeal
And of their great escape.
When finished she had turned to Rick
Who stared with mouth agape.

Then Rick took Jill into his arms
So he could reassure
Her history had no bearing
And his intentions pure.

For a moment Jill knew comfort
And found a sense of peace.
Although she knew it could not last
It had been nice to lease.

The Assault

They walked towards the facility
With vengeance in their eyes.
Their stride made clear what's their intent
With no wish to disguise.

They were defiant in their stride
With purpose plain to see.
They had come for retribution
And the facility.

Jill thought the Major sympathized
With what was done to them.
Where his response would be restrained
So, placed her faith in him.

From a distance the Major saw
The Squad in their approach.
And he saw that they meant business
The closer they'd encroach.

He ordered his men to stand down
And not to interfere.
Those coming truly dangerous
Whom they should not go near.

The Major saw Skye flash a sign
They should evacuate.
The Squad may not take prisoners
So, his men should vacate.

When Cross had seen the exodus
He knew something was wrong.
For the Major military
Who, also, was headstrong.

Cross then begged for his protection
Which the Major ignored.
He hoped Cross got what he deserved
As he, the man abhorred.

Cross saw they would abandon him
And leave him to his fate.
He then yelled to them they're cowards
As they slipped out a gate.

Cross wondered what had made them run
That's clearly on its way.
That would cause the military
To simply back away.

As the door they had thrown open
All seven had fanned out.
Where they'd clear the facility
And opposition rout.

Cross was overcome with panic
Not knowing what he faced.
It's clear the Major had a clue
The way his men had raced.

That's when Cross called to his aides
Protection he would need.
Whomever breached the outer walls
They needed to impede.

The girls a liability
Of which he must dispose.
With their presence a certainty
The project they'd expose.

Cross ordered aides to kill them all
Because he had not known
They're about to face a whirlwind
From seeds already sown.

His men were merely sitting ducks
Who quickly were dispatched.
They swept through the facility
With fierceness that's unmatched.

When Chris had come upon the girls
She first asked if okay.
They told her of Page's demise
For which Cross had to pay.

While Jill and Brie had both paired up
Jill found she was amused.
For Brie would captivate the men
Whom next she had abused.

They knew exactly who she was
And of her were afraid.
For the one who stood before them
Had been the one called Jade.

Half of those that Jade approached
Had turned to run away.
But found there had been no escape
If marked to be Jade's prey.

They recklessly had charged at Skye
Because she seemed so frail.
To find perceptions can deceive
As Skye put them through hell.

While Kat and Lynn also paired up
To go in search of Cross.
Although they calmly neutralized
Any they came across.

Until they came to Doctor Cross
Who begged they spare his life.
He had claimed he'd been misguided
When Chris had pulled a knife.

Chris was off the reservation
As vengeance she had sought.
For all the things they'd done to her
She had grown quite distraught.

But Jill then stepped tween Cross and Chris.
Chris ordered Jill to move.
The bastard had been worse than Blank
And stain she would remove.

Skye said that they were damaged goods
But not damaged that way.
It's what they wished to make of them
Which had not been okay.

Though Chris had slowly backed away,
The knife she still had held.
Skye slowly had come up to her
Where vengeance she dispelled.

Jill then asked Brie to take the girls
And round up Cross' men.
Then deliver to the Major
To be placed in a pen.

While they dealt with Chris' meltdown
Lynn and Kat disappeared.
Who moved through the facility
With purpose engineered.

Though Cross was now their prisoner,
They showed him no respect.
The man had been a murderer
And showed the girls neglect.

The seven walked out through the door
Grown tired of the mind games.
Behind them the facility
Erupted into flames.

They smiled at the finality
As they watched the place burn.
They hoped they'd put an end to it
Where it could not return.

The Aftermath

Jade had carried Page's body
From the facility.
The other girls had stood and cried
In abject misery.

Some of the girls troops had restrained
When Cross had first appeared.
And then when Cross was led away
Even the soldiers jeered.

When Cross given to the Major,
His thanks had been profuse.
For they had done what he could not
And ended the abuse.

They did not wait for the police
As questions they'd avoid.
The girls were left with the Major
In trust they'd fill the void.

Though Cross and his associates
Had blamed the Mantis Squad.
But because they'd been a secret,
Police had thought them odd.

Debbie Lynn, in particular,
Had shown no gratitude.
As though it had been owed to her
Had seemed her attitude.

The Fire

While the fire had burned for hours
And raged out of control.
A crowd had gathered at the site
To watch flames lap and roll.

The government had disavowed
That it had been involved.
The building was not one of its,
So of guilt it's absolved.

Neighbors began to speculate
What the building contained.
They already were suspicious
What in it was retained.

It had an air of secrecy
That clearly was defined.
Where renovations that were made
Were meant to outside blind.

While even now engulfed in flames
The mystery remained.
What purpose had the building served
And what had it contained?

The Trial

Though the trial had been more lengthy
Than many would have thought.
The outcome was a certainty
Where justice had been sought.

Although the one who pulled the strings
They still had not yet caught.
For Cross would not identify
The other one they sought.

The girls and parents testified
To what Cross put them through.
What punishment prescribed for him
He, clearly, had been due.

The Major, too, had testified
To all that he had seen.
While someone else responsible
That as yet, went unseen.

The verdict had been no surprise
The moment it was read.
For Cross was guilty on all counts
To serve till he was dead.

Parting Ways

One last time the seven gathered
So they could say goodbye.
While bound by their experience
Some had begun to cry.

All seven were forever scarred
In light of their ordeal.
The trauma of experience
With which they had to deal.

Blank believed their abilities
Had been a gift from God.
The teens, however, disagreed
Thinking it made them odd.

Most hated their abilities
Which had set them apart.
The reason Blank had chosen them
To in her scheme take part.

Blank's plan an abomination
It had one good outcome.
It had brought them all together
Where friends they had become.

They thought it time they parted ways
As project was no more.
No other girl would suffer what
Was hid behind that door.

So, with a hug each said goodbye
Then turned and walked away.
The Mantis Squad had been dissolved
Which each had thought okay.

Within the Shadows

In a remote corner office
A new plan underway.
The shadows that protected him
Had never given way.

As a plotter and a schemer,
Never held to account
For all of his bad decisions
And projects he would mount.

There had been few that knew his name
As loner he had been.
So entrenched in the government
Elections just a din.

The Mantis Squad he may have feared
If they had known of him.
Though he thought they should be grateful
That he created them.

If the project had shown success
They all would know his name.
With his team of skilled assassins
True power he could claim.

For each rung that hung above him
He would eliminate.
Until he reached the highest heights
Which he thought was his fate.

This had only been a setback
That he would overcome.
For he worked within the shadows
Assured of his aplomb.

Epilog

Though Rick and Jill had parted ways,
They had done so as friends.
For Jill joined the academy
In hope to make amends.

While Kat and Lynn found wedded bliss
Which had been more their style.
They were done with adventuring
Which they'd thought juvenile.

While Jade and Chris both moved away
And not heard from again.
Jill hoped their issues were resolved
And not like hers had been.

Skye became a psychiatrist
Who dealt with people's needs.
She found she was quite good at it
With her perceptive reads.

Although Brie became a madam
Where skills were put to use.
Who became a wealthy woman
Though offered no excuse.

www.ingramcontent.com/pod-product-compliance
Lightning Source LLC
Chambersburg PA
CBHW020322130626
46549CB00003B/974

* 9 7 9 8 8 9 1 9 4 5 7 5 3 *